American STREAMLINE

BERNARD HARTLEY & PETER VINEY
CONNECTIONS

Workbook B

Units 41–80

American adaptation by Flamm/Northam Authors and Publishers Services, Inc.

Oxford University Press

Oxford University Press

200 Madison Avenue
New York, N.Y. 10016 USA

Walton Street
Oxford OX2 6DP England

OXFORD is a trademark of
Oxford University Press.

ISBN 0-19-434117-8 (Workbook A)
ISBN 0-19-434118-6 (Workbook B)
ISBN 0-19-434115-1 (Complete Student Book)
Copyright © 1984 B. Hartley, P. Viney,
and Oxford University Press

First published 1984

Printing (last digit): 15 14 13 12 11 10

Illustrations by Paddy Mounter

Printed in Hong Kong

To the teacher

Workbook B of *American Streamline: Connections* consists of forty units. Each unit relates directly to the corresponding unit in *American Streamline: Connections* Units 41–80.

The *Workbook* is an optional component of the course, designed to provide language summaries and additional written exercises. It may be used in the following ways:

1. In more extensive courses as additional classroom material, providing extra oral practice and written reinforcement and consolidation of the basic core material in the Student Book.

2. As material for homework in more intensive situations.

The *Workbook* should only be used after full oral practice of the corresponding unit in the student's edition. The language summaries provide material for review.

Another workbook is available for units 1–40 of the student's edition, under the title *Workbook A.*

Bernard Hartley
Peter Viney

Unit 41

He's the man. I saw him.	He's the man I saw.
She's the woman. I met her.	She's the woman I met.
That's the coat. He was wearing it.	That's the coat he was wearing.
They're the people. I saw them.	They're the people I saw.

Exercise 1

A. *He's the man I saw.*
B. *That's the gun he was carrying.*
C. *They're the gloves he was wearing.*
D. *They're the boots he was wearing.*
E. *That's the money he stole.*

Continue.

A. ....

....

B. ....

....

C. ....

....

D. ....

....

E. ....

....

A. ....

....

B. ....

....

C. ....

....

D. ....

....

E. ....

....

Exercise 2

He's the man. I saw him. *He's the man I saw.*

Continue.

1. He's the man. She married him.

....

2. She's the woman. He loves her.

....

3. They're the children. She teaches them.

....

4. That's the car. She drives it.

....

5. They're the windows. He's broken them.

....

6. She's the doctor. I spoke to her.

....

7. That's the bank. They robbed it.

....

8. Those are the people. We helped them.

....

Unit 42 (Review)

Exercise 1

Complete this.

1. shake	shook	shaken	**5.** bite	....	....	**9.** find	....	....
2. hide	hid	hidden	**6.**	chose	....	**10.**	flew	....
3.	....	kept	**7.**	....	broken	**11.** bleed	....	....
4.	tried	....	**8.**	fell	....	**12.** take	....	....

Exercise 2

I've been smoking too much.
You shouldn't smoke so much.
Continue.

1. He's been drinking too much coffee.

....

2. She's been working too hard.

....

3. They've been drinking too much beer.

....

4. We've been worrying too much.

....

5. She's been telling too many stories.

....

Exercise 3

He wanted breakfast. He went downstairs.
He went downstairs for breakfast.

Continue.

1. He wanted advice. He went to the doctor.

....

....

2. He needed a rest. He went to Nantucket.

....

....

3. She wanted the plates. She went to the kitchen.

....

....

Exercise 4

Look at the student's book. Fill in the blanks.

Jerry Streisen almost .... a nervous .... last year. His
.... told him to .... a few days off. He went to Nantucket,
and .... late in the evening. Mrs. Searcy, the .... of the house,
.... him to his room. At nine o'clock the
.... morning Jerry went .... for breakfast. Jerry met Catherine,
the landlady's thirteen-year .... daughter. There were four ....
at the table, one for Mrs. Searcy, one for Catherine, one for Jerry and an ....
place. Jerry asked .... the empty place. Catherine .... him a
strange .... about her father. "My father disappeared three years
.... when he was fishing. My mother .... he'll come
.... so she .... his breakfast .... morning. That's
my father's .... on the wall."

The story .... Jerry, and when Mrs. Searcy returned and
.... four cups of tea, he .... even more nervous. Suddenly the
door .... and the man in the picture walked .... the room.
Jerry jumped .... and ran .... of the room. Catherine's father
.... understand, but he knew that Catherine was a good storyteller. Catherine just
laughed.

Unit 43

Language Summary

How long	have you has she	been doing that?

How much How many	have you has she	done?
How far	have you	driven?

Exercise 1

All of these people are on vacation in Disney World. Look at this information. It's nine-thirty now.

Name	Starting Time	Activity	Number
Toshio Ito	8:00	writing postcards	seven postcards
Laura Diaz	9:00	shopping (buying souvenirs)	several souvenirs
Dennis and Clara Woll	8:30	visiting exhibits	four exhibits
Lisa Pucci	9:15	taking pictures	about twenty
Harry Kovacs	8:15	reading	three short stories

Look at the example, and do the same.

Toshio Ito
1. **A:** *What's he doing?*
   B: *He's writing postcards.*
2. **A:** *How long has he been writing postcards?*
   B: *He's been writing postcards since eight.*
3. **A:** *How many has he written?*
   B: *He's written seven.*

Laura Diaz

1. **A:** ....

   B: ....

2. **A:** ....

   B: ....

3. **A:** ....

   B: ....

Dennis and Clara Woll

1. **A:** ....

   B: ....

2. **A:** ....

   B: ....

3. **A:** ....

   B: ....

Lisa Pucci

1. **A:** ....

   B: ....

2. **A:** ....

   B: ....

3. **A:** ....

   B: ....

Harry Kovacs

1. **A:** ....

   B: ....

2. **A:** ....

   B: ....

3. **A:** ....

   B: ....

Exercise 2

he/typing/two hours/nine letters
He's been typing for two hours. He's done nine letters.

1. I/using this book/a long time/forty-three units

....

2. they/writing/an hour/all their homework

....

Unit 44

Language Summary

She's the woman. I met her. . . . She's the woman I met.
She's the woman. She met me. . . . She's the woman that met me.

Exercise 1

Look at these famous people.

One of them wrote a famous play.
One of them went to the moon in a spaceship.
One of them composed a famous piece of music.
One of them painted a famous picture.

A. *Shakespeare is the one that wrote a famous play.*
B. Hamlet *is the play he wrote.*

Continue.

1. A. Leonardo da Vinci ....

....

B. ....

....

2. A. Neil Armstrong ....

....

B. ....

....

3. A. Tchaikovsky ....

....

B. ....

....

Exercise 2

He's the doctor. He did the operation. *He's the doctor that did the operation.*
That's the camera. She used it. *That's the camera she used.*
Continue.

1. That's the horse. It won the race.

....

2. That's the exam. They've passed it.

....

3. They're the people. The helicopter rescued them.

....

4. That's the volcano. It erupted.

....

5. That's the house. He rents it.

....

6. She's the movie star. He's going to interview her.

....

7. That's the food. He cooked it.

....

Unit 45

He's the teacher | *that* | *'s been teaching me.*
 | *who* |

Look at this:

Punctuation

.	period
,	comma
"Hello"	quotation marks
?	question mark
!	exclamation mark
ABC	capital letters
You've	apostrophe
:	colon

Exercise

This is the letter that John wrote to Mary. Write it again with punctuation and capital letters.

167 woodley road cleveland ohio 44101 usa september 10 dear mary thanks for your letter ive got some good news ill be able to come to mexico city next month im worried about hotels what was the name of the hotel you used to stay at there are a lot of things i want to see in mexico city the cathedral the anthropological museum the aztec pyramids and the national university are you at school all day i hope not do you remember bill king hes the one whos studying spanish at cleveland college hes been giving me some lessons he says i should buy a cassette player so i can listen to real spanish voices maybe my spanish will be better than yours see you soon hasta luego all my love john

Unit 46

Exercise 1

Complete this conversation.

A: Can I help you?

B: ....

A: Which concert?

B: ....

A: Which day?

B: ....

A: Which performance?

B: ....

A: Where would you like to sit?

B: ....

A: Here's a seating plan of the concert hall.

B: ....

A: $25.

B: ....

A: $15.

B: ....

A: Thank you. Here are your tickets.

Exercise 2

Complete this conversation.

A: Good morning.

B: ....

A: Yes, we've still got a few left.

B: ....

A: Yes. Yes, it is.

B: ....

A: The times are on the poster over there.

B: ....

A: If you like. Cash or credit card?

B: ....

Exercise 3

Complete this conversation.

A: Hello. Dino's Italian Restaurant.

B: ....

A: Yes. What time?

B: ....

A: O.K. How many people?

B: ....

A: Oh, well, we can put some tables together.

Unit 47

Language Summary

I | like | reading.
 | don't like | swimming.

Do you like reading?

I'm | afraid of | doing that.
 | tired of |
 | interested in |

Exercise

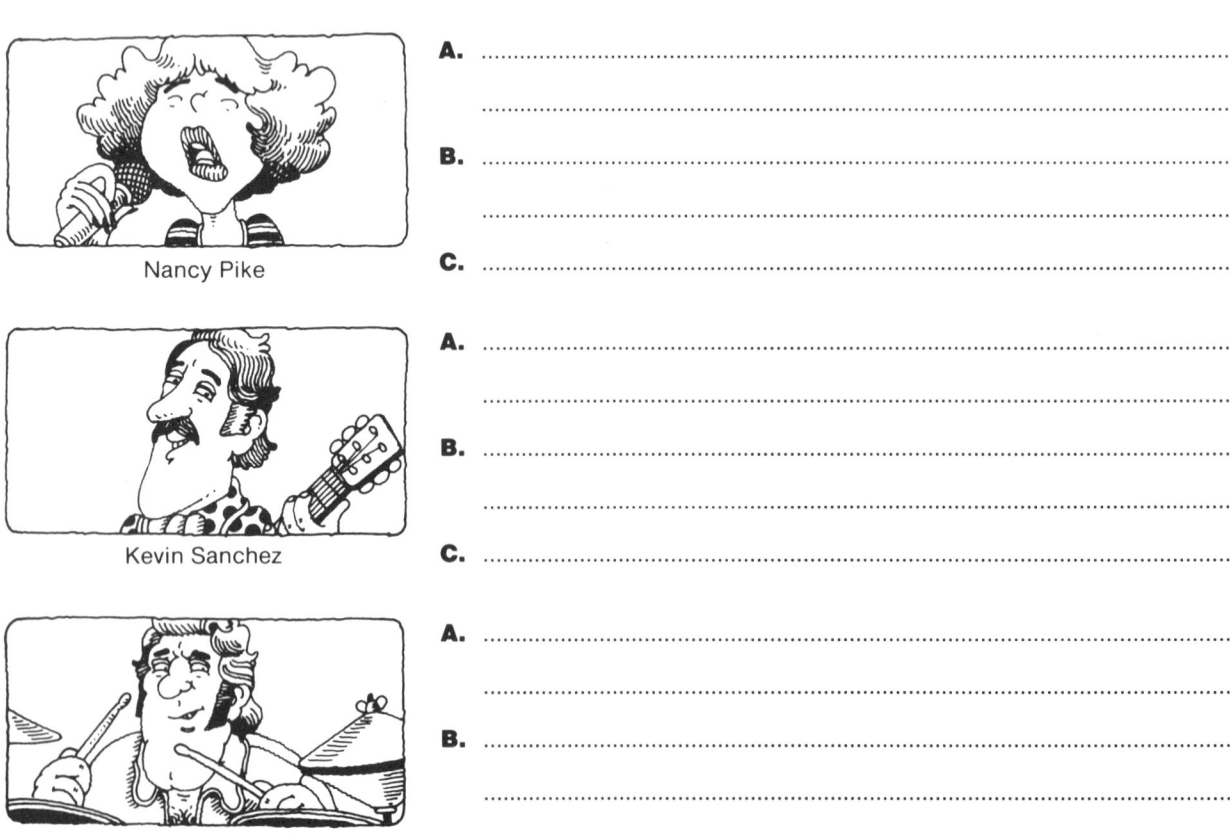

MELODY MAGAZINE   September 19th

POP GROUP INFORMATION THIS WEEK—*"THE FUZZ"*

NAME	AGE	LUCKY NUMBER	FAVORITE COLOR	LIKES	DISLIKES	FEARS
Nancy Pike *Lead vocalist*	19	7	red	opera camping tennis	smoking cooking	getting old
Kevin Sanchez *guitar, synthesizer*	21	2	gold	electronic music spending money new clothes	washing dishes paying taxes	being poor
Ron Colman *bass guitar*	20	5	green	modern jazz going to discos expensive restaurants	staying at home television	flying
Biff Hastings *drums*	29	13	gray	opera boxing fast cars	getting up early shaving	going to the dentist

Ron Colman

A. *He likes listening to modern jazz.*
He likes going to discos and eating in expensive restaurants.
B. *He doesn't like staying at home.*
He doesn't like watching television.
C. *He's afraid of flying.*

Nancy Pike

A. ....
....
B. ....
....
C. ....

Kevin Sanchez

A. ....
....
B. ....
....
C. ....

Biff Hastings

A. ....
....
B. ....
....
C. ....

Unit 48

Language Summary

It may rain.
We | *might* | *go to Pennsylvania.*
    | *might not* |

What will the weather be like in Texas?
. . . during | *the morning/the afternoon/*
            | *the evening/the night.*

Exercise 1

Where's San Francisco? It's on the West Coast.   *Where's Seattle? It's in the Northwest.*

Write eight questions and answers.

1. ....

2. ....

3. ....

4. ....

5. ....

6. ....

7. ....

8. ....

Exercise 2

Look at the weather forecast for the area around Washington, D.C. in the student's book.
Look at the weather map above and write a forecast for the whole United States.

....

....

....

....

....

....

....

....

....

Exercise 3

he/movies/disco
He might go to the movies, or he might go to a disco.

Continue.

1. they/stay home/go out ....

   ....

2. she/television/radio ....

   ....

3. he/football/tennis ....

   ....

4. I/tea/coffee ....

   ....

5. we/fly/drive ....

   ....

Unit 49

Language Summary

How much is there?	How many are there?	He's getting upset.	Start	doing something.
There's	some.	There are	some.		Begin	
	a little.		a few.			
	too much.		too many.			
	enough.		enough.			
	a lot/lots of . . .		a lot/lots of . . .			
	plenty.		plenty.			

Exercise 1

he/cook/ten minutes ago   *He's cooking now. He started cooking ten minutes ago.*
Continue.

1. they/play football/at three o'clock ....

2. she/drive/an hour ago ....

3. we/shop/after lunch ....

4. I/write/five minutes ago ....

5. he/work/at nine o'clock ....

6. you/read/ten minutes ago ....

7. it/rain/three hours ago ....

8. she/study English/in December ....

9. john/type/at 10:30 ....

10. it/rain/this morning ....

Exercise 2

In the U.S. there's plenty of farm land, and there are plenty of colleges.
But there isn't enough oil, and there aren't enough prisons.

Write eight sentences about your country.

1. ....

2. ....

3. ....

4. ....

5. ....

6. ....

7. ....

8. ....

Exercise 3

He's watching a movie on TV. It isn't interesting.   *He's getting bored.*
Continue. You can use these words: hungry/tired/worried/upset/thirsty/cold.

1. She hasn't eaten for six hours.
....

2. She's waiting for a friend at the air-port. The plane is late, and there's no news.
....

3. They've been working all day. It's very late.
....

4. It's a very hot day. He hasn't drunk anything for two hours.
....

5. She's told him to do it three times.
....

6. The food was hot. It's been on the table for twenty minutes.
....

Unit 50

Exercise 1

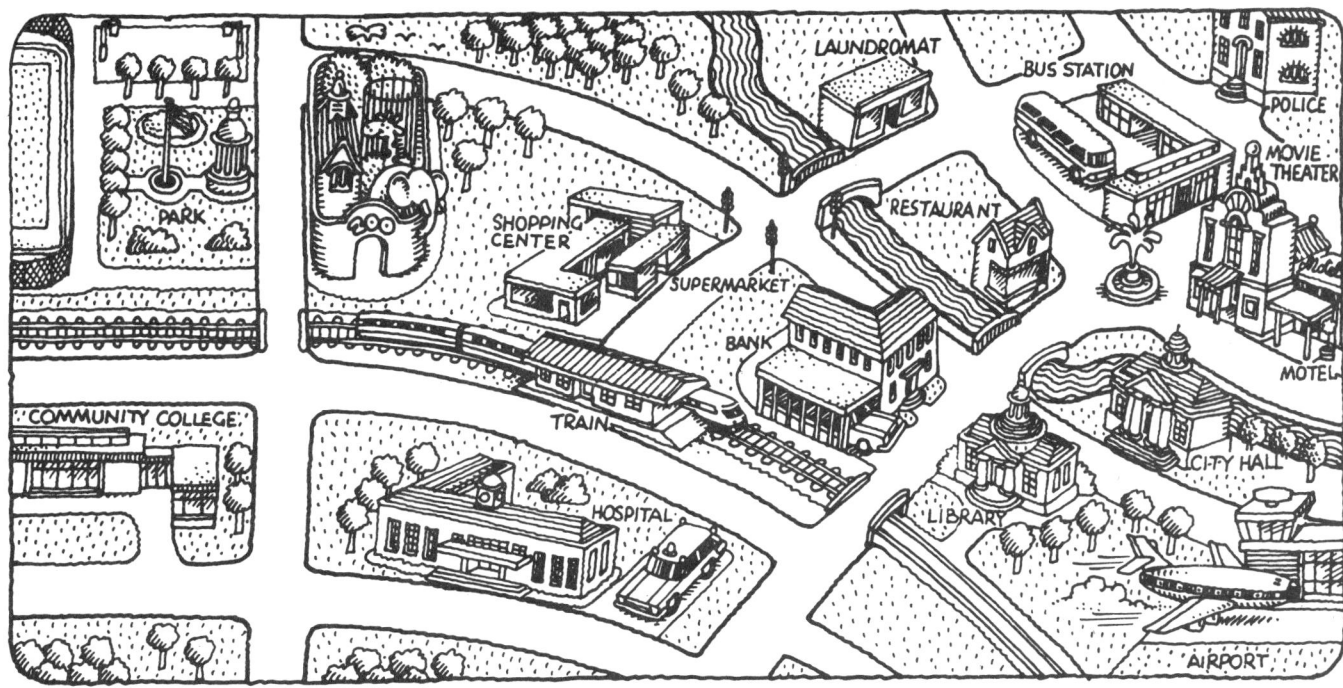

Follow the route on the map, and answer the questions.

Walk out of the police station, turn left, take the first street on the right, go around the fountain, and straight ahead. What can you see on your right? .... Cross the bridge, and you will see a road to your left. What can you see at the end of the road? .... Don't turn left, go straight ahead. What's on your right? .... What's on your left? .... Go over the bridge, and take the second right. Continue to the intersection. Which building have you passed? .... Turn right, and continue across the bridge. What's over on your left? .... Go past the park, and turn right. What can you see on the right? .... At the light turn left. Stand on the bridge. Look right. What can you see? .... Take the second right. Where are you? ....

Exercise 2

You've just come out of the hospital. Write directions to the supermarket.

....

....

....

....

Exercise 3

You're going to draw a picture.
Draw two hills across the top of the picture.
The sun is shining in the top left-hand corner.
There's an old house on the hill on the right.
Draw a road from the old house to a modern house in the bottom left-hand corner.
There's a river across the middle of the picture.
Draw a bridge where the road goes over the river.

Unit 51

Ask him if he's married. Are you married?
Ask him where he lives. Where do you live?

There's a big crowd on Perry Street. They're looking at a man who's standing outside a window on the sixth floor. A police officer is at another window. He's holding a radio and talking to a police captain on the street. The captain wants him to continue talking to the man for as long as possible. They know nothing about the man, and they need to know as much as possible.

Exercise 1

Captain (Capt.): Ask him what his name is.
Police Officer (P.O.): *What's your name?*

Continue.

Capt.: Ask him where he's from.

P.O.: ....

Capt.: Ask him where he works.

P.O.: ....

Capt.: Ask him if he's married.

P.O.: ....

Capt.: Ask him if he has any children.

P.O.: ....

Capt.: Ask him if he wants to speak to anybody.

P.O.: ....

Exercise 2

Capt.: *Ask him if he feels all right.*
P.O.: Do you feel all right?

Continue.

Capt.: ....

P.O.: Why are you there?

Capt.: ....

P.O.: How long have you been there?

Capt.: ....

P.O.: Have you been drinking?

Capt.: ....

P.O.: How long are you going to stay there?

Capt.: ....

P.O.: Are you going to jump?

Capt.: ....

P.O.: Do you want to die?

Capt.: ....

P.O.: Why do you want to die?

Unit 52

Do you know	*what it is?*	*I don't know*	*what it is.*
Do you have any idea	*if it's yours?*	*I have no idea*	*if it's yours.*
I wonder	*if he works here?*		*if he works there.*

The police found this woman earlier today. She was sleeping in a train station. She doesn't have any identification with her. Her clothes are expensive, but they look old and dirty. She can't remember anything about herself. She's lost her memory.

Exercise 1

P.O.: Now what's your name?
Woman: *I have no idea what my name is.*
P.O.: Are you married?
Woman: *I'm sorry. I don't know if I'm married.*

Continue.

P.O.: Where do you live?

Woman: ....

P.O.: How old are you?

Woman: ....

P.O.: Do you have any children?

Woman: ....

P.O.: Where did you work?

Woman: ....

P.O.: Where were you born?

Woman: ....

P.O.: Which school did you go to?

Woman: ....

P.O.: Have you ever been in the hospital?

Woman: ....

P.O.: How did you hurt your head?

Woman: ....

P.O.: Did you have an accident?

Woman: ....

P.O.: When did you lose your memory?

Woman: ....

Exercise 2

Look at Exercise 1.
This is the police officer's report. Complete it.

Middleburg Police Department

REPORT   Date:_____

We found a woman at 6:00 this morning. She has no idea what her name is.

Unit 53

Language Summary

Ms. Pat Laine, who lives in Oceanside Cliffs, went home.
Small boats, which are carrying detergent, are racing to the scene.

Exercise 1

Pat Laine lives in Oceanside Cliffs. She went home.
Ms. Pat Laine, who lives in Oceanside Cliffs, went home.

Continue.

1. The *S.S. Titan* is a supertanker. It crashed into a cargo ship.

....

....

2. Ms. Laine lost her house. She is sleeping in a hotel.

....

....

3. The thief stole a van. He's in for a surprise.

....

....

Small boats are carrying detergent. They are racing to the scene.
Small boats, which are carrying detergent, are racing to the scene.

4. The house was on the edge of a cliff. It fell into the ocean.

....

....

5. The van belonged to the San Diego Zoo. It contained two boxes of snakes.

....

....

6. The local residents are spending the night in a school. They are afraid to go home.

....

....

Exercise 2

Look at the story in the student's book. Use these words and write another story.

"SHOCK FOR A THIEF"
Somewhere/Chicago/thief/horrible shock. Yesterday evening/someone/truck/Fairmont Road. truck/Zingle Brothers Circus. inside/large box. it/gorilla. truck/Midway Airport/circus. thief/truck/driver/coffee shop/sandwich to go.

....

....

....

....

....

Exercise 3

Fill in the blanks in this story.

"WHERE'S MY CAR?"

Mr. Joseph Simmons, ... lives in Watertown, came .... of a local bar last .... and couldn't .... his car. It .... on the top .... a hill, and .... the evening it rolled .... the hill and fell .... the river. He forgot .... put the brake on!

Exercise 4

E	O	A
D	G	S
R	N	U

How many words can you make? You can use all the letters. It's possible to make one nine-letter word.

....
....
....
....
....
....
....

Unit 54

Language Summary

The street was empty except for Sara Garcia . . . There was nobody else.
The room was empty except for a chair . . . There was nothing else.
All the hotels were closed, except for one . . . There was nowhere else.

Look at this:

young	bald				fat	pretty
middle-aged	with	curly	hair		thin	good-looking
old/elderly (polite)		long			big	handsome
with a beard		short			tall	beautiful
a mustache		straight			short	ugly
glasses		light			average height	
		dark				
		blonde				
		gray				

Exercise 1

Look at the example. Look at the language above. Describe the other people.

AGE : 24. HEIGHT : 5ft. 7in.   AGE : 24 HEIGHT : 5ft. 9in.   AGE : 76. HEIGHT : 5ft. 3in.   AGE : 42. HEIGHT : 5ft. 5in.

He's a handsome young man. He's of average height with short, dark hair and a mustache.

1. ....

2. ....

3. ....

Exercise 2

Now describe yourself and your teacher.

S. ....

T. ....

Exercise 3

The street was empty except for Sara Garcia. *There was nobody else.*

Continue.

1. His pockets were empty except for a pen. ....

2. The restaurants were closed except for one. ....

3. The beach was empty except for Sue and Janet. ....

Unit 55

Language Summary

I	'll won't will will not	leave	when before after as soon as	she comes.
We	'll	wait	until	she comes.

Exercise 1

Judy Spencer is a new flight attendant. This is her schedule for tomorrow's flight to San Francisco.

11:25 demonstrate oxygen masks
Before she demonstrates the oxygen masks, she'll check the seat belts.
After she demonstrates the oxygen masks, she'll take her seat for the take off.

Continue.

1. ....
....

2. ....
....

3. ....
....

4. ....
....

5. ....
....

Streamline Air

Instructions For Cabin Crew
Flight: 271
From: New York (La Guardia) **To:** San Francisco

11:20   check seat belts
11:25   demonstrate oxygen mask
11:30   take seat for take off

11:40   rent earphones
11:55   serve beverages
12:30   serve lunch

1:00   pick up lunch trays
1:30   start movie
1:35   count beverage money

4:00   pick up earphones
4:20   prepare to land
4:35   say good-bye to passengers

6. ....
....

Look at this:

{ We'll get there. Then we'll have a sandwich.
{ When we get there, we'll have a sandwich.

{ We'll get there. We'll have a sandwich immediately.
{ As soon as we get there, we'll have a sandwich.

Exercise 2

get to the airport/check luggage
As soon as he gets to the airport, he'll check his luggage.

Continue.

1. go through security check/go into waiting room

....
....

2. they/call flight/board the plane

....
....

3. get on plane/fasten seat belt

....
....

Exercise 3

get off plane/wait for luggage
When he gets off the plane, he'll wait for his luggage.

Continue.

1. pick up luggage/rent a car

....
....

2. leave airport/drive to hotel

....
....

3. get to hotel/register

....
....

Unit 56

Language Summary

| I | 'll
will
won't | do this | if | you | do
don't do | that. |

Bruce and Rachel are planning their vacation. They've looked at a lot of brochures. They're interested in the package tours to Puerto Rico and Hawaii, but they can't decide. They might go to Puerto Rico, or they might go to Hawaii.

Exercise 1

If they go to Puerto Rico, they'll stay for seven days.
Continue.

Seven days in Puerto Rico with

AmericanAirlines

- See Old San Juan
- Enjoy beautiful beaches and fabulous food
- Free plane trip to St. Thomas (Virgin Islands)

Choice of hotels:	(including airfare)
Condado Inn	$481
Depot Plaza	$428
Moro Castle Hotel	$409

1. .... American Airlines.

2. .... Old San Juan.

3. .... beautiful beaches.

4. .... fabulous food.

5. .... St. Thomas.

Exercise 2

If they stay at the Condado Inn, it'll cost them $481.
Write two sentences.

1. ....

2. ....

Exercise 3

Complete the advertisement below. Use this information: eight days/United Airlines/Hawaii/super surfing/oriental food/bus trips/other beaches.

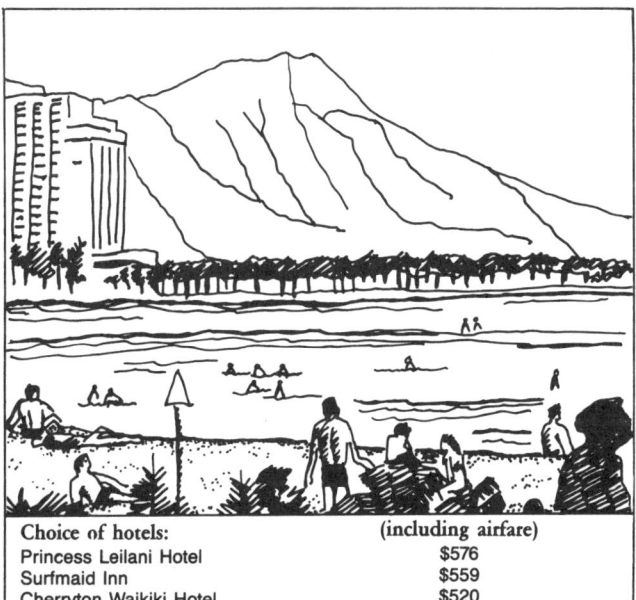

Choice of hotels:	(including airfare)
Princess Leilani Hotel	$576
Surfmaid Inn	$559
Cherryton Waikiki Hotel	$520

Exercise 4

Look at Exercise 1 above.
Write six sentences that begin: *If they go to Hawaii . . .*

1. ....

....

2. ....

....

3. ....

....

4. ....

....

5. ....

....

6. ....

....

Exercise 5

Look at Exercise 2 above. Write three sentences about a vacation in Hawaii.

1. ....

2. ....

3. ....

Unit 57 (Review)

Exercise 1

Complete this.

1. choose   chose   chosen

5. bleed ....

9. shake ....

2. fight   fought   fought

6. ....   kept   ....

10. ....   hid   ....

3. lie   lay   lain

7. strike ....

11. ....   made

4. ....   stole   ....

8. stick ....

12. ....   bitten

Exercise 2

Grand Prix Racing				1st prize $200,000		
Florida Grand Prix		Miami		2nd prize $100,000		
				3rd prize $ 50,000		
				4th prize $ 25,000		

DRIVER	NATIONALITY	AGE	CAR	PRACTICE TIME	POSITION IN LAST RACE	FORM
Rodrigo Cabral	BR	40	Renault ELF Turbo	1 min. 25.81 sec.	Second	World Champion 1975, 1976, 1977, 1980
Carlos Villa	CO	36	Spirit-Honda	1 min. 24.85 sec.	Third	World Champion 1981, 1982
Mario Rivera	I	29	Ferrari	1 min. 26.10 sec.	First	World Champion 1983
Jimmy Sullivan	US	38	Arrows-Ford	1 min. 26.82 sec.	Fourth	World Champion 1978
KEY	BR = Brazil		CO= Colombia	I = Italy	US = United States	

The Florida Grand Prix is a very important race. Four drivers are very close in the World Championship table. Look at the diagram. Look at the example. Write about the other drivers.

Rodrigo Cabral

Cabral is Brazilian. He's forty years old, and he's driving for the Renault team. He had the second-best time in practice. He was second in his last race. If he's second in this race, he'll win $100,000. He has been world champion four times. If he wins this race, he may be world champion again.

....

....

....

1. Carlos Villa

....

....

....

....

3. Jimmy Sullivan

....

....

....

....

....

....

....

2. Mario Rivera

....

....

Unit 58

Exercise 1

These are some of the signs used on roads in the United States. Look at the example. Look at the expressions in the box. Put the correct ones under the signs.

divided highway ends	railroad crossing	men working on road
steep hill	slippery road	falling or fallen rocks
wild animals	no U-turn	children
traffic light ahead	two way traffic ahead	school
hospital to right	no left turn	pedestrian crossing

1. *Pedestrian crossing.*

2. ....

3. ....

4. ....

5. ....

6. ....

7. ....

8. ....

9. ....

10. ....

11. ....

12. ....

13. ....

14. ....

15. ....

Exercise 2

A	B
If you park in the wrong place ...	... you'll get a flat tire.
If you drive too fast ...	... the engine will overheat.
If you drink and drive ...	... you'll have an accident.
If you don't put water in the radiator ...	... you'll get a speeding ticket.
If you don't drive carefully ...	... you'll lose your license.
If you drive over broken glass ...	... you'll get a parking ticket.

If you don't drive carefully, you'll have an accident.

Now make five other sentences.

1. ....

2. ....

3. ....

4. ....

5. ....

Unit 59

Look at this:

Letters

Beginnings	Endings
Beginnings	*Endings*
Dear Sir:	Yours sincerely,
Dear Madam:	Yours truly,
Dear Sir or Madam:	
Dear Mr. Smith:	Yours sincerely,
Dear Mrs. Smith:	Sincerely yours,
Dear Miss Smith:	
Dear Ms. Smith:	
Dear John,	Sincerely,
Dear Mary,	Best wishes,

If you want to send money by mail, you write:

I enclose a | check | for ($10).
            | money order |

Exercise 1

Look at the rates and write a letter to reserve a room for four nights. Send $35 as a deposit. Write your address, the date, and your signature.

Lighthouse Motel

Rates

Single room	$35
Single room with kitchenette	$45
Ocean view room	$55
Ocean view room with kitchenette	$65

All rooms have double beds and cable TV.

Exercise 2

Here is a reply from the hotel to Faye Bass. Write it on the letter with the correct punctuation.

august 21 1983 ms faye bass 1812 orange avenue lubbock texas 79401 dear ms bass thank you for your letter of august 8 we confirm your reservation for the nights of august 26–30 could you please send $35 as a reservation fee we are sure you will enjoy your stay in gulf shores yours sincerely angela martin manager

Lighthouse Motel
675 Gulf Breeze Drive
Gulf Shores, Alabama 36143
Telephone (205) 387-4141

Unit 60

Language Summary

I, You He, She We, They	'd had hadn't had not		seen	it.		Had	I, you, he, she we, they	seen	it?	Yes, I had. No, I hadn't.

Exercise 1

Jay Power is the manager of a small company. Last week he took a one-day business trip. He left these instructions for his staff. When he came back, he was upset with all of them!

Janice hadn't finished the annual report.

Write six sentences.

1. ....

2. ....

3. ....

4. ....

5. ....

6. ....

> **MEMO**
>
> | To: | Office staff |
> |---|---|
> | From: | Jay Power |
> | Date: | May 7 |
> | Subject: | Instructions for May 8
I'll be out of the office
tommorrow. |
> | Janice: | finish annual report |
> | Helen: | type letters |
> | Chris: | photocopy new price lists |
> | Harry: | check accounts |
> | Yolanda: | process orders |
> | Roberta: | mail price lists |
> | Sam: | write April sales report |

Exercise 2

Last week Redwood College played a basketball game in another city. The Redwood "Tigers" stayed at a hotel, and the coach gave them instructions the night before the game. The next day the "Tigers" lost 96-53. Nobody had obeyed the coach's instructions!

They had eaten too much.

Write six sentences.

1. ....

2. ....

3. .... **5.** ....

4. .... **6.** ....

> **Redwood College Tigers**
>
> 1. Don't leave the hotel.
> 2. Don't stay up late.
> 3. Don't eat too much.
> 4. Don't have beer with dinner.
> 5. Don't smoke.
> 6. Don't go to the bar.
> 7. Don't talk to reporters.

Exercise 3

Answer these questions. Before you started this course . . .

1. Had you studied any English? ....

2. Had you learned any English words? ....

3. Had you seen any movies in English? ....

4. Had you read any books in English? ....

5. Had you met any Americans? ....

6. Had you met any British people? ....

7. Had you heard any records in English? ....

8. Had you been to an English-speaking country? ....

9. Had you studied any other language? ....

10. Had you seen any TV programs in English? ....

Unit 61

It happened <u>when</u> I had just finished college.
<u>When</u> I arrived, they had gone into class.
<u>As soon as</u> I had parked the car, I rushed back to the bank.

Exercise 1

9:00 The president arrived.
The plane took off.

A: *What happened when the President arrived?*
B: *When the President arrived the plane took off.*

Continue.

9:00 The teacher arrived. The class started.
9:10 Annie arrived.   9:00 The class started.

A: ....

B: ....

C: ....

D: ....

7:15 The President sat down. The conference began.
7:20 The Vice-President arrived.   7:15 The conference began.

A: ....

B: ....

C: ....

D: ....

8:10 Mary Smith arrived.
8:00 The plane took off.

C: *What happened when Mary Smith arrived?*
D: *When Mary Smith arrived the plane had taken off.*

8:00 The director took his seat. The movie began.
8:30 Diane walked into the theater.   8:00 the movie began.

A: ....

B: ....

C: ....

D: ....

7:30 The guests sat down. Mrs. Gonzalez served dinner.
8:00 I got to the party.   7:30 Mrs. Gonzalez served dinner.

A: ....

B: ....

C: ....

D: ....

Exercise 2

Fill in the blanks.

My .... embarrassing experience .... when I had just .... an

expensive .... in a restaurant. I had .... finished the meal when the waiter

.... the bill. I .... my hand in my ...., and my wallet ....

there! My ....book wasn't there either. Then I remembered! Before I..................

home, a button .... fallen off my .... I .... changed my jacket,

but I had ....my money in the other jacket!

Unit 62

Language Summary

I, You	'd	been	reading	for	a long time.
He, She	had				two hours.
We, They	hadn't			since	six o'clock.
	had not				Monday.

How long | had | he | been | reading?

I did it myself.   *We made it ourselves.*
Do it yourself!   *You did it yourselves.*
He saw it himself.   *They'd seen it themselves.*
She's seen it herself.

Exercise 1

He got to the bus stop at eleven o'clock. The bus came at 11:15.
He'd been waiting for fifteen minutes when the bus came.

Continue.

1. They sat down at 7:30. The waiter brought the menu at eight o'clock.

....

2. The house started burning at midnight. The fire fighters got there at 12:20.

....

3. She began typing at nine o'clock. The boss came in at ten.

....

4. Joe Freezer began boxing twelve years ago. Last month he became world champion.

....

5. The Dallas Cowboys started playing at three o'clock. They scored the first touchdown at 3:30.

....

Exercise 2

He was watching TV when it happened.
How long had he been watching TV?

Continue.

1. They were sitting in the restaurant when the police arrived.

....

2. She was working in Denver when she met him.

....

3. He was living in Ecuador when it happened.

....

Exercise 3

She never buys bread at the supermarket. *She makes it herself.*

Continue.

1. No one helped them to paint the house.

....

2. There are a lot of shelves in the kitchen. He likes making shelves.

....

3. Nobody helped them to decorate the kitchen.

....

4. Nobody helped him to do anything!

....

Unit 63

| It's | made of | gold. |
| They're | | |

Exercise 1

These shoes are made of leather.
This shirt's made of cotton.

Look at the words in the box. Write six sentences.

shoes	gold
necklace	cotton
socks	wood
sweater	plastic
doors	leather
comb	silver
shirt	wool
rings	nylon

1. ....
2. ....
3. ....
4. ....
5. ....
6. ....

Exercise 2

TOP TEN ALBUMS

This Week	Last Week		
1	(15)	**WALK IN SPACE**	The Fuzz
2	(2)	**LIFE'S BEEN SWEET TO ME**	Rob Dillon
3	(1)	**BANG YOUR HEAD AGAINST A WALL**	The Rats
4	(7)	**WE'VE GOT TO HELP EACH OTHER**	Marvyn Soul
5	(3)	**ROCK 'N' ROLL PARTY**	Shining Teeth
6	(6)	**MY KENTUCKY SWEETHEART**	Daisy Barton
7	(4)	**CONNECTIONS & DEPARTURES**	The Smash
8	(12)	**IF YOU LEAVE ME I'LL BE SORRY**	Cathy Tree
9	(5)	**PRETTY LITTLE DISCO DANCER**	Groove
10	(29)	**I DID IT ALL MYSELF**	Frank Sonata

"Walk in Space" is first this week.
It was fifteenth last week.
Write sentences about the records which are this week's
number 2,3,5,7,8, and 10.

1. ....
....
2. ....
....
3. ....
....
4. ....
....
5. ....
....
6. ....
....

Exercise 3

"Walk in Space" has gone up fourteen places.
"Rock 'n' Roll Party" has gone down two places.
"My Kentucky Sweetheart" hasn't moved.

Write sentences about the other seven records in this week's Top Ten.

1. ....
2. ....
3. ....
4. ....
5. ....
6. ....
7. ....

Look at this:

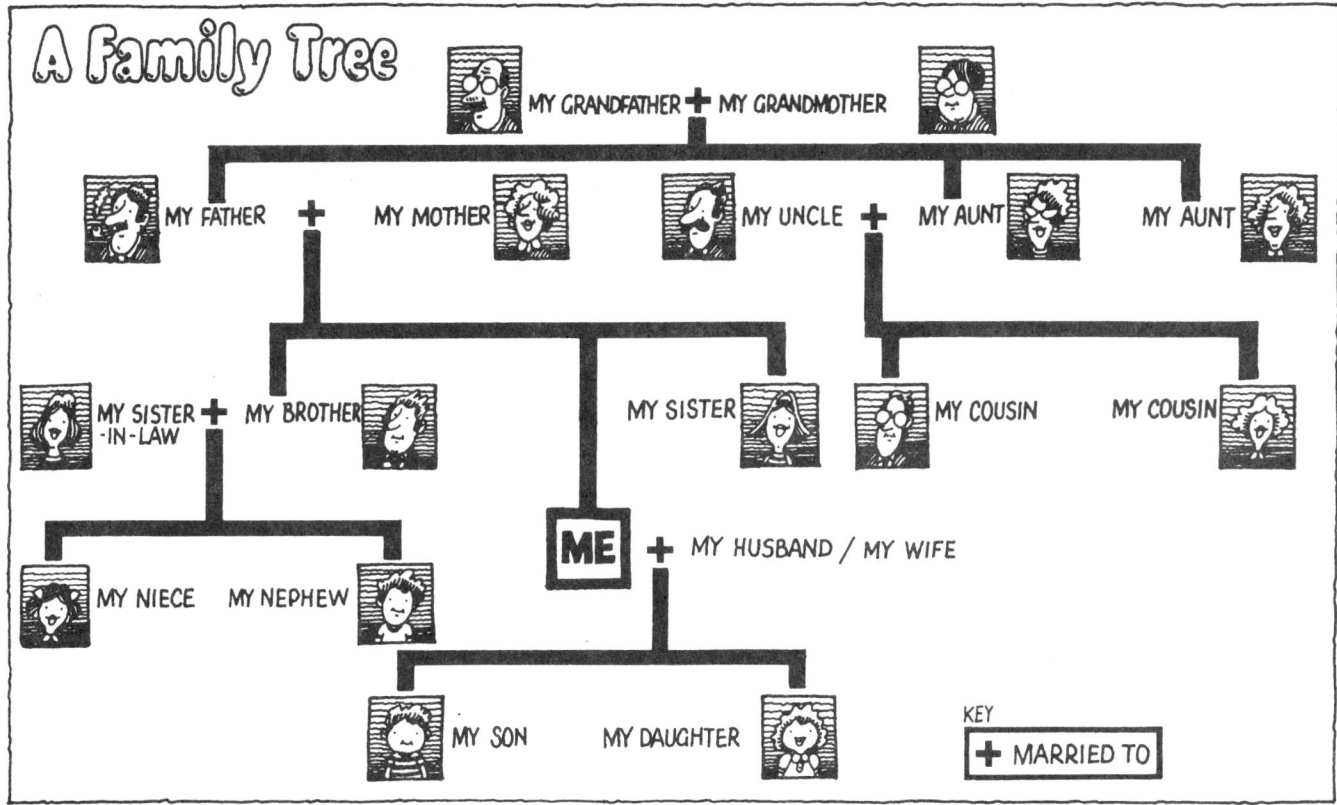

Exericse 4

Now make your family tree. You can write names in. You may need these extra
words: brother-in-law/father-in-law/mother-in-law/son-in-law/daughter-in-law
grandson/granddaughter.

Exercise 5

Fill in the blanks in this conversation.

A. I'm looking for a birthday present for ....

B: How old is ....?

A: ....

B: What about ....?

A: No, I bought .... last year.

B: What about ....?

A: No, ... already got ....

B: Then, what about ....?

A: Yes, what .... made of?

B: ....

A: Fine. How much .... ?

B: ....

Unit 64

It	is	made in	the U.S.
	was	produced in	
They	are	imported from	
	were	exported to	

It	was	invented	by	her.
		discovered		
		written		
		made		

Exercise 1

Where was your watch made? It was made in Switzerland.
Write questions and answers with: radio/shoes/pen/camera/jeans.

1. ....

2. ....

3. ....

4. ....

5. ....

Exercise 2

In the United States:
A. *Fords are made in Michigan.*
B. *Wine is exported from California.*
C. *Copper is imported from Chile.*

Now write sentences about your country, three with "made," three with "exported," and three with "imported."

1. **A.** ....

   B. ....

   C. ....

2. **A.** ....

   B. ....

   C. ....

3. **A.** ....

   B. ....

   C. ....

Exercise 3

Tropical fruit is produced in Puerto Rico.
Soybeans are produced in the United States.
Write six sentences about your country.

1. ....

2. ....

3. ....

4. ....

5. ....

6. ....

Exercise 4

Indira Gandhi	created	in	London.
The telephone	won	by	Strauss.
Charlie Chaplin	produced	by	Washington.
"The Blue Danube" waltz	made	in	Alexander G. Bell.
Mickey Mouse	born	in	Walt Disney.
Penicillin	discovered	by	Honduras.
Abraham Lincoln	written	by	Shakespeare.
Toyotas	born	in	Alexander Fleming.
The 1978 World Cup	composed	in	Japan.
Bananas	killed	by	Argentina.
Romeo and Juliet	invented	by	India.

Charlie Chaplin was born in London.

Write ten more sentences.

1. ....

2. ....

3. ....

4. ....

5. ....

6. ....

6. ....

7. ....

8. ....

9. ....

10. ....

Unit 65

It	is was has been will be	done.	Is Was	it		done?
			Has	it	been	
			Will		be	

Exercise 1

Gloria Navarro is the owner of the Lighthouse Motel. She has hired a new manager because she doesn't want to manage the motel every day. She wants to enjoy life now. It's 10:45 now. She's checking with the manager. Look at these conversations.

A. Ms. Navarro: *Have the bills been prepared?*
Manager: *Yes, they have.*
Ms. Navarro: *When were they done?*
Manager: *They were done at seven o'clock.*

B. Ms. Navarro: *Have the lunch menus been typed?*
Manager: *No, they haven't. Not yet.*
Ms. Navarro: *When will they be done?*
Manager: *They'll be done at 11:00.*

Now write six conversations—three like A and three like B.

1. Ms. Navarro: ....

   Manager: ....

   Ms. Navarro: ....

   Manager: ....

2. Ms. Navarro: ....

   Manager: ....

   Ms. Navarro: ....

   Manager: ....

3. Ms. Navarro: ....

   Manager: ....

   Ms. Navarro: ....

   Manager: ....

4. Ms. Navarro: ....

   Manager: ....

Lighthouse Motel
Gulf Shores, Alabama 36143

WORK SCHEDULE   Date: July 9TH

7:00 prepare the bills
8:00 clean the swimming pool
9:30 make the beds
10:00 clean the kitchenettes
10:30 clean the coffee shop
11:00 type the lunch menus
11:30 fix broken stairs
11:45 set up tables for lunch
12:00 check reservetions

   Ms. Navarro: ....

   Manager: ....

5. Ms. Navarro: ....

   Manager: ....

   Ms. Navarro: ....

   Manager: ....

6. Ms. Navarro: ....

   Manager: ....

   Ms. Navarro: ....

   Manager: ....

Exercise 2

Look at the work schedule for the Lighthouse Motel.

The bills are usually prepared at seven o'clock.

Write five sentencés.

1. ....

2. ....

3. ....

4. ....

5. ....

Unit 66

Language Summary

It	is	being	done.
They	are		
It	had	been	
They			

Someone did that. .... It was done.
Someone does that. .... It is done.
Someone is doing that. .... It is being done.
Someone has done that. .... It has been done.
Someone had done that. .... It had been done.
Someone will do that. .... It will be done.

Exercise 1

Complete this.

1. spread   spread   spread   **5.** .... chosen   **9.** .... sent

2. shoot   shot   shot   **6.** .... fought ....   **10.** break ....

3. wind   wound   wound   **7.** .... lain   **11.** bore ....

4. panic   panicked   panicked   **8.** .... run   **12.** .... built

Exercise 2

This is 006, the secret agent. He's very worried. He's on an important mission.
He's speaking to headquarters now. The operator is telling "M," his boss, what's happening.

SOMEONE'S FOLLOWING ME!

SOMEONE'S FOLLOWING HIM. HE DOESN'T KNOW WHO IT IS – BUT HE'S BEING FOLLOWED!

Now write what the operator is saying.

SOMEONE'S OPENING MY LETTERS!

1. ....
....

SOMEONE'S WATCHING MY APARTMENT!

2. ....
....

SOMEONE'S LISTENING TO MY PHONE CALLS!

3. ....
....

SOMEONE'S RECORDING MY CONVERSATIONS!

4. ....
....

SOMEONE'S FOLLOWING MY CAR!

5. ....
....

Exercise 3

When 006 got back to his apartment, the door was open!
Someone had broken the lock!

He didn't know who had broken it, but it had been broken!

Continue.

1. Someone had stolen his gun!

....

....

2. Someone had taken his passport!

....

....

3. Someone had broken the window!

....

....

4. Someone had put a poisonous snake in his bed!

....

5. Someone had searched his room!

....

6. Someone had emptied his drawers!

....

Exercise 4

Someone sent 006 on the mission.
He was sent on the mission.

Continue.

1. Someone contacts him every day.

....

2. Before he left, someone had given him a gun.

....

3. Someone is following him everywhere.

....

4. Someone has broken into his apartment three times!

....

5. Someone will meet him tomorrow in a coffee shop.

....

6. They will give him instructions.

....

Exercise 5

006 has just sent back this report about his assistant, Agent 003.
Fill in the blanks.

TOP SECRET REPORT

TO M   DATE April 13th
SUBJECT Secret Agent 003   SIGNED *006*

Agent 003 is dead. He was.........in the river. Nobody
knows.........killed him, or why.........killed.
He had been.........three times in the back. He......
just met some.........in a coffee shop. He......
the coffee shop with them. The gun has not........
found yet. The river is.........searched by the police.
I am very worried. I think the killers were looking for me.

Unit 67

Language Summary

It | can be | done.

WAR IN SPACE

Produced by Frank Forbes Cupola
Directed by Joseph Ducas
Written by H.G. Bell
Music composed by John Williamson
and played by the San Diego
Symphony Orchestra

NOW SHOWING *Empire Theatre Times Square*

Neighborhood theaters starting next week

Exercise

1. *It was produced by Frank Forbes Cupola.*
2. *It was directed by Joseph Ducas.*
3. *It was written by H.G. Bell.*
4. *The music was composed by John Williamson.*
5. *It was played by the San Diego Symphony Orchestra.*
6. *It's being shown at the Empire Theater on Times Square.*
7. *It can be seen at neighborhood theaters starting next week.*

Continue.

Staying Ahead

Produced by Talia Shriner

Directed by Sly Stallion

Written by Tony Stallion

Music composed by Andy Gibson and played by The Gibson Brothers

Now showing **TransAm Theater on Third Avenue**

Other major cities starting next Friday

1. ....
2. ....
3. ....
4. ....
5. ....
6. ....
7. ....

Wildlife of the Earth

Written by Margot Gramer
Illustrated by Tim Ching
Photos taken by Debra Sistino

Printed in full color by Oxbow Books

PUBLISHED NEXT MONTH

1. ....
2. ....
3. ....
4. ....
5. ....

TONY CHENILLE'S GREATEST HITS

Recorded live at the RAINBOW THEATER

Produced by: Pat Rothman
Piano: Daryl Dragon
Bass: Jose Vargas
Drums: Ted Duke

Toni accompanied by Melissa Chenille

All songs written by Tony Chenille

1. ....
2. ....
3. ....
4. ....
5. ....
6. ....
7. ....

Unit 68

Language Summary

He became popular.
She became his wife.

{ *He went to Hollywood. He made several movies there.*
{ *He went to Hollywood where he made several movies.*

Charlie Chaplin—Career of a clown

1889	April 16th, born in London.
1896	First appeared on stage. Age seven.
1908	One of the most popular entertainers in England.
1910	First went to the USA.
1913	Went to Hollywood. Made his first movie. Made thirty-five comedies in first year. Developed character of "the tramp" with bowler hat, mustache, out-turned feet, walking cane and baggy trousers.
1915	Joined Essenay Studios for $1,250 a week. Made fourteen movies in one year.
1916	Worked for Mutual Films. Made $670,000 in one year.
1917	Married Mildred Harris, (divorced 1920). Joined First National for $1 million for eight movies, as producer, scriptwriter, director, and star.
1919	Formed United Artists.
1921	Visited Europe. Was met by large crowds everywhere.
1924	Married Lita Grey.
1925–31	Made three of his best movies—*The Gold Rush*, *The Circus*, and *City Lights*. Didn't speak in a movie until 1936 *(Modern Times)* and then only sang one song.
1936	Married Paulette Goddard (divorced 1942).
1943	Married Oona O'Neill. Lived in USA 1913–1952. Never became a U.S. citizen.
1952	Moved to Switzerland. Unpopular in USA because of his political opinions.
1957	Went to England. Made *The King in New York*. Not shown in the USA.
1966	To England again. Made *Countess from Hong Kong* with Sophia Loren.
1972	Returned to Hollywood. Was given an Oscar.
1975	Went to London. Was knighted by the Queen. (Became "Sir Charles Chaplin, K.B.E.").
1977	December 25th, died Vevey, Switzerland. Buried Corsier.

Exercise 1

1913 Went to Hollywood. Made his first film.
He went to Hollywood where he made his first film.

Write eight sentences.

1. 1915 ....

2. 1916 ....

3. 1918 ....

4. 1921 ....

5. 1957 ....

6. 1966 ....

7. 1972 ....

8. 1975 ....

Exercise 2

1896 (7) First appeared on stage. Age seven.
He first appeared on stage when he was seven.

Write six sentences using: 1910 (21), 1913 (24), 1919 (30), 1943 (54), 1972 (83), 1977 (88).

1. ....

2. ....

3. ....

4. ....

5. ....

6. ....

Exercise 3

Mildred Harris became his wife in 1917.
Write three more sentences about his wives.

1. ....

2. ....

3. ....

Exercise 4

He became one of the most popular entertainers in England in 1908.
Write sentences with: rich and famous, never/U.S. citizen, an Oscar winner, Sir Charles Chaplin.

1. ....

2. ....

3. ....

4. ....

Exercise 5

Answer these questions.

1. When was he born?

....

2. Where was he born?

....

3. What nationality was he?

....

4. Where did he make most of his movies?

....

5. How many times was he married?

....

6. Why did he leave the USA?

....

7. Where did he die?

....

8. Where is he buried?

....

Exercise 6

Look at the picture. Describe "The Tramp."

....

....

....

Unit 69

9780194341189

Language Summary

If	I	had enough money	I	'd	buy a new car.
		could drive		would	
		were rich			
What	would	you	do,	if	you	had	enough money?
						were	rich?

Exercise 1

Marie wants to buy a car, but she doesn't have enough money. *If she had enough money, she'd buy a car.*
Continue.

1. They want to take a vacation, but they don't have enough time.

....

2. Sandra wants to change her job, but she doesn't have the qualifications.

....

3. He wants to make a phone call, but he doesn't have the correct change.

....

4. They want to listen to the football game, but they don't have a radio.

....

Exercise 2

Ray wants to go to the concert, but he can't get a ticket. *If he could get a ticket, he'd go to the concert.*
Continue.

1. Kate wants to work as a secretary, but she can't type well.

....

2. Tom wants to live in the U.S., but he can't get a visa.

....

3. They want to go to the game, but they can't get tickets.

....

4. She wants to get a job in France, but she can't speak French.

....

Exercise 3

They want to buy a new TV, but it's too expensive. *If it were cheaper, they'd buy a new TV.*
Continue.

1. He wants to get a suntan, but it's too cold.

....

2. She wants to rent a car, but she's too young.

....

3. They want to answer the questions, but they're too hard.

....

4. She wants to apply for the job, but she's too young.

....

Unit 70

Language Summary

I'd have the steak if I were you. or *If I were you, I'd have the steak.*

Exercise 1

A: *What would you like for an appetizer?*
B: *I can't decide between the soup and the asparagus.*

Write two more conversations.

1. A: ....

   B: ....

2. A: ....

   B: ....

Exercise 2

A: *What should I have—the minestrone soup or the fresh asparagus?*
B: *If I were you, I'd have the asparagus.*

Write three more conversations.

1. A: ....

   B: ....

2. A: ....

   B: ....

3. A: ....

   B: ....

Today's Specials

Appetizers

Minestrone soup	$2.50
Fresh asparagus	$3.50

Entrees

Chicken in red wine	$8.00
Roast leg of lamb	$10.00

Desserts

Strawberry cheesecake	$3.00
Chocolate cream pie	$2.00

Beverages

House wine	$4.00 a carafe
(red or white)	$1.50 a glass

Look at this:

boiled .... cooked in water
steamed .... cooked over boiling water
fried .... cooked in oil or fat in a pan
stewed .... cooked slowly in a little liquid

baked .... cooked in an oven without fat or oil
roasted .... cooked with fat in an oven
grilled .... cooked over radiant heat
broiled .... cooked under radiant heat

Exercise 3

Now write a short menu with specialties from your region or country.

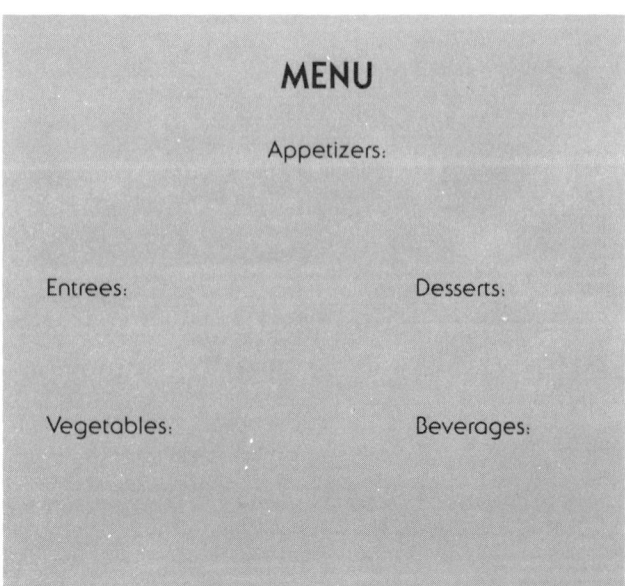

MENU

Appetizers:

Entrees:

Desserts:

Vegetables:

Beverages:

Exercise 4

A friend from the U.S. is coming to your town. Use your menu and write five sentences suggesting things to him.

If I were you, I'd have the . . .

1. ....

....

2. ....

....

3. ....

....

4. ....

....

5. ....

....

Unit 71

Language Summary

| If | I | were Governor,
could choose, | I | 'd
would
wouldn't
would not | spend money on highways. |

Would you spend money on highways? Yes, I would/No, I wouldn't.

Exercise 1

A state Governor is meeting with the cabinet to discuss public spending for next year. They all have notes. The Governor is speaking to the Commissioner of Education.

Governor: *Well, what would you do?*
Commissioner: *I'd spend more money on teachers' salaries. If we had higher salaries, we could have better teachers. If we had better teachers, children would learn more.*

> **EDUCATION**
> higher teachers' salaries
> — better teachers
> — children learn more

Now answer for each commissioner.

> **COMMERCE**
> attract more businesses to state
> — more jobs
> — more unemployment

1. **A.** ....
   B. ....
   C. ....

> **HEALTH**
> New hospitals
> — healthier people
> — more productivity

2. **A.** ....
   B. ....
   C. ....

> **TRANSPORTATION**
> more farm-to-market roads
> — farmers produce more
> — cheaper food

3. **A.** ....
   B. ....
   C. ....

> **TAXATION & FINANCE**
> increase taxes on cigarettes and liquor
> — more money
> — could reduce personal taxes

4. **A.** ....
   B. ....
   C. ....

> **ENERGY**
> increase gasoline tax
> — people drive less
> — less pollution

5. **A.** ....
   B. ....
   C. ....

> **CORRECTIONS**
> more jails and prisons
> — keep more criminals behind bars
> — less crime and violence

6. **A.** ....
   B. ....
   C. ....

Exercise 2

I wouldn't spend money on new hospitals.

Write four things <u>you</u> wouldn't spend money on.

1. ....

2. ....

3. ....

4. ....

Unit 72

Exercise 1

Imagine that you are going to a desert island. You can take an animal, a book, a record, a can of something, a bottle of something, and three other things. What would you take?

1. ....

2. ....

3. ....

4. ....

5. ....

6. ....

7. ....

8. ....

Exercise 2

If I had a lot of money, I would take a long vacation.

Write six things that you would do.

1. ....

2. ....

3. ....

4. ....

5. ....

6. ....

Exercise 3

If you weren't here, where would you like to be?
If I weren't here, I'd like to be in Honolulu.

Now write answers.

1. If you could be someone else, who would you like to be?

    ....

2. If you weren't studying English, which language would you study?

    ....

3. If you could have a new first name, what would you choose?

    ....

4. If you could choose your job, what would you be?

    ....

5. If you could have any car, which kind would you have?

    ....

6. If you could eat anything you wanted tonight, what would you eat?

    ....

7. If you could meet anyone in history, who would you like to meet?

    ....

Unit 73

Someone	will must can might could should	do that.	It	will must can might could should	be done.	They	will must can might could should	do that.	It	won't mustn't can't might not couldn't shouldn't	be done.

In many parts of the world there is famine—there isn't enough food or water—and people are dying. Sometimes this is because of changes in climate, sometimes it's because of earthquakes or volcanic eruptions, sometimes it's because of wars. When this happens in a country, it isn't enough to send money. There are short-term needs (immediate) and long-term needs (for the future). Look at these things and put them into two lists.

feed babies	send doctors and nurses	train doctors and nurses
send food	build temporary housing	send medicines
build bridges	provide agricultural equipment	plant seeds
send trucks	send fertilizer and pesticides	teach farmers
build hospitals	send blood plasma	send farm animals
send blankets	construct roads	build schools
send helicopters	introduce irrigation systems	

Add to your lists anything that <u>you</u> think would be needed.

Immediate Needs (short-term needs)	**Future Needs** (long-term needs)
feed babies	*build schools*

Now look at your lists. Look at the two examples.
Babies must be fed immediately.
Schools should be built, but they can't be built yet. They can be built later.

Now write sentences like these using your lists.
Use a separate sheet if you need to.

A. Immediate Needs

....

....

....

....

....

....

B. Future Needs

....

....

....

....

....

Unit 74

Language Summary

Maria said, "This is my bag." .... She said that was her bag.
Maria said, "These aren't my pens." .... She said those weren't her pens.
John said, "I like tea." .... He said he liked tea.
John said, "I don't like coffee." .... He said he didn't like coffee.
Anne said, "I can dance well." .... She said she could dance well.
Anne said, "I can't cook." .... She said she couldn't cook.
Paul said, "I have a new apartment." .... He said he had a new apartment.
Paul said, "My wife doesn't have a car." .... He said his wife didn't have a car.
Mary said, "I've been to France." .... She said she'd been to France.
Mary said, "My mother hasn't been there." .... She said her mother hadn't been there.
Mike said, "I bought it last week." .... Mike said he had bought it the week before.
Mike said, "I didn't buy it yesterday." .... Mike said he hadn't bought it the day before.
Jean said, "I'll do it tomorrow." .... Jean said she would do it the next day.
Jean said, "I won't do it next week." .... Jean said she wouldn't do it the next week.

Look at this:

When you are reporting something you may have to change these words.

this...that   today...that day   this week...that week
these...those   yesterday...the day before   last month...the month before
here...there   tomorrow...the next day   next year...the next year
now...then

Exercise 1

Complete this.

He heard *Rob Dillon was in Detroit.*

1. I read ....
....

2. I saw ....
....

3. She said ....
....

Exercise 2

These people were interviewed at different airports last week.
Write reports of what they said.

1. London airport: Tracy Barker,
tennis player.

This is my first visit to England.
I'm going to play at Wimbledon.
I've trained very hard.
I want to win.
I have a good chance.
I won the U.S. Open last
month.
I'll be in England for three weeks.

....
....
....
....
....
....
....
....

2. New York airport: Diana Rich,
movie star.

It's nice to be home again.
I've come to make a new movie.
My children will be here next week.
My husband won't be with me.
I'm going to divorce him.
We don't love each other any more.
I sold my house in Hollywood last month.
I can't tell you any more.

....
....
....
....
....
....
....
....

3. Baltimore airport: Alan Wolfe,
who was arrested last week.

I don't want to say much.
I haven't spoken to my lawyer yet.
The stories about me aren't true.
I didn't steal the money.
I've never stolen anything.
I can't understand the newspaper reports.
I'm not a criminal.
I'm just an ordinary person.
I won't answer any more questions.

....
....
....
....
....
....
....
....
....

Exercise 3

Complete this.

HE SAID HIS NAME WAS JOHNNY RABID.

SHE SAID HE PLAYED IN A PUNK ROCK GROUP.

SHE SAID SHE HAD KNOWN HIM FOR THREE DAYS.

SHE SAID THEY HAD MET THE WEEK BEFORE.

SHE SAID THEY WERE GOING TO GET MARRIED.

HER FATHER SAID HE WOULDN'T COME TO THE WEDDING!

Unit 75

Language Summary

She asked me | *what my name was.*
| *if I was a secret agent.*

006, the secret agent, has just returned from his mission. He
was arrested and questioned. They asked him these twenty questions.

1. Do you speak English?
2. What's your real name?
3. Why do you have two passports?
4. Who do you work for?
5. Are you a secret agent?
6. Why are you carrying a gun?
7. Has it been fired?
8. Have you contacted anybody here?
9. How did you enter the country?
10. Have you been here before?

11. Is anybody with you?
12. When did you enter the country?
13. Why are you here?
14. Why don't you have a visa?
15. Why are you carrying $25,000?
16. Did you bring the money with you?
17. When will you leave the country?
18. Who killed the man in your hotel room?
19. Will you work for us?
20. Why won't you work for us?

Exercise 1

006 had to report to his boss.

They asked if I spoke English.
They asked what my real name was.

Continue.

1. ....

   ....

2. ....

   ....

3. ....

4. ....

5. ....

6. ....

7. ....

8. ....

9. ....

10. ....

11. ....

12. ....

13. ....

14. ....

15. ....

16. ....

17. ....

18. ....

Unit 76

Exercise 1

Lucy Price works for World Travel. She's interviewing someone who wants to work for them.
Look at the application form. She put an asterisk (*) where she asked a question.

She asked what his name was, and he said it was Chris Zois.

World Travel, Inc.

Application Form
*Job: *Tour guide*
*Name: *Chris Zois*
*Address: *475 Henderson Drive, Walnut, California*
*Place of birth: *Sandusky, Ohio*

EDUCATION: LANGUAGES:
*☑ High School   * ☐ French   ☐ Portuguese
*☑ College   * ☑ Spanish   ☐ Chinese
                    * ☐ Italian   *☑ Japanese
*Countries visited (No.): Countries worked in:
14   * Japan   *Mexico

*Experience (as guide):   Present job:
Wings Travel, 1980   *Flight Attendant,
East-West Tours, 1982   Capitol Air

*Other experience: Other qualifications:
Waiter, 1979   *Member, U.S. Tour
Actor, 1981   Guide Association

1. ....

2. ....

3. ....

4. ....

5. ....

6. ....

7. ....

8. ....

9. ....

10. ....

11. ....

12. ....

13. ....

14. ....

15. ....

Exercise 2

She asked what his name was. *What's your name?*
Continue.

1. She asked where he lived.

....

2. She asked how old he was.

....

3. She asked if he was married.

....

4. She asked how long he had been married.

....

5. She asked if he had any children.

....

6. She asked if he could drive.

....

7. She asked if he would be able to travel.

....

8. She asked if he liked traveling.

....

9. She asked if he smoked.

....

10. She asked why he wanted to change his job.

....

Unit 77

Language Summary

I'm going to have	*my car tuned up.*
I've just had	*my suit cleaned.*
I had	*my shoes fixed.*
I should have	*my coat lengthened.*

Nan Vogel has just picked up her car from the garage. She's had the car tuned up.

She's had the brakes tested.
Write six sentences.

1. ....
2. ....
3. ....
4. ....
5. ....
6. ....

AUTO SERVICE CENTER **Middleburg**

Name: Ms. N. Vogel Date: Aug. 12
Tune-up checklist: Mechanic: Reilly

test brakes	✔	**Bill:**
fill radiator	✔	Parts: $ 4.00
check battery	✔	Labor: $ 75.00
change oil	✔	Sub-total: $ 79.00
rotate tires	✔	Tax: $ 6.32
test lights	✔	**Total:** $ 85.32

Exercise 2

Mr. and Mrs. Allen have just bought an old house in the country. It isn't in very good condition. They can't do the work themselves, and they've made a list of things to have done.

They're going to have the roof fixed.
Write six sentences.

1. ....
2. ....
3. ....
4. ....
5. ....
6. ....

Fix roof.
Put in central heating.
Rewire house.
Repaint exterior.
Restore interior walls.
Put in new windows.
Change Door.

Exercise 3

Herb is forty. He wants to get some life insurance. The agent has just given him a list to take to his doctor, because he has to have a medical examination.

You should have your chest X-rayed.
Write four sentences.

1. ....
2. ....
3. ....
4. ....

Exercise 4

Now write three things that you are going to have done in the near future.
For example, *I'm going to have my hair cut next Saturday.*

1. ....
2. ....
3. ....

NATIONAL PYRAMID LIFE
INSURANCE CO.

test eyes
check blood pressure
check heart
examine throat
X-ray chest

Unit 78

Fill in the blanks.

1. Every Tuesday .... Jessica makes a cake. .... Tuesday while she was .... the cake, her five .... old .... Andrew .... watching her. She .... just put some flour, ... butter, ... sugar, and two eggs into the bowl when .... phone .... She .... Andrew not .... touch anything and went to .... it.

2. It .... her husband, Stuart, on the .... He said that he .... be home early. Andrew likes .... in the .... and he wanted .... help with the .... He picked .... a large .... from the shelf.

3. While his mother .... still .... to his .... Andrew emptied the .... into the .... and mixed .... together. His mother .... back and asked .... he .... touched anything. He said he .... She finished .... the cake, ... the mixture into a cake pan and put it in the ....

4. That night .... dinner, Jessica brought Stuart .... of coffee. She said she had .... his favorite .... and went to .... it. Stuart said it smelled .... and Jessica said Andrew .... helped .... to make it. Stuart smiled. When he .... the cake, his .... disappeared. Jessica .... him .... the matter .... and then .... Andrew why he .... laughing.

Unit 79

Look at these people:

Sergio Caldas
Chef

Monty Hunter
Taxi driver

Mick Turpin
Boxer

1. *"I wear a white hat at work."*

1. ....

....

....

1. *"I have to train very hard."*

2. ....

2. ....

2. ....

3. ....

3. ....

3. ....

4. ....

4. ....

4. ....

5. ....

5. ....

5. ....

6. ....

6. ....

6. ....

7. ....

7. ....

7. ....

Now look at these twenty-one sentences. Two of them have been written
into the columns above. Read all the sentences carefully and put
them in the correct columns in the same way as the examples.

✓ He said he wore a white hat at work.
He said he had to carry a lot of change.
He said he didn't have many teeth.
He said he drove very carefully.
He said he was worried about gas prices.
He said he would open his own restaurant one day.
He said his nose had been broken several times.
He said he never drove a car on his days off.
He said he was a famous person.
He said he knew every street in Chicago.
He said he had several assistants.

He said he would retire at thirty-six.
He said he wore shorts when he was working.
✓ He said he had to train very hard.
He said he had learned his job in Paris.
He said he washed his hands several times a day.
He said he had heard some very interesting
  conversations.
He said he had never been knocked out.
He said he often worked at night.
He said he worked every evening.
He said he had never served canned food in his life.

Unit 80

Exercise

Write a letter to a pen-pal. Write your address and today's date. Begin "Dear Anne ..." Tell her what your name is. Tell her how old you are and what nationality you are. Tell her where and when you were born. Describe yourself. Tell her what you do (where you work or what you are studying). Tell her what you would like to do. Describe your house, then tell her about your family. Tell her what you like doing, what you are interested in and what you don't like doing. Tell her about your town, (how big it is, how many movie theaters there are, etc.). Ask her to write to you. Ask her to tell you about herself. Sign the letter "Sincerely."

International Pen Pals

Write to people in the U.S.

Send a letter to:
American Sharing Program
Route 1
Box 798
Beaverton, Oregon 97007

Review

Fill in the blanks.

Unit

41. He was wearing a .... and carrying a ....

42. Catherine had .... eyes (2 words).

43. The driver bought .... (2 words).

44. Anne was never .... in Spanish class.

45. Mary's bought a .... cassette player.

46. The Bay Area Tour takes .... hours.

47. Jeff lives .... with his parents (2 words).

48. Pittsburgh is in .... Pennsylvania.

49. The waitress said she .... never dropped a plate.

50. Cosmetics are on the .... (2 words).

51. The doctor told the paramedic not to .... the man on the beach.

52. Do you think the police would .... them?

53. There were two boxes of .... snakes.

54. The door had a .... above it (2 words).

55. The First Lady will visit .... places in Middleburg.

56. The pot was .... on the little boy's head.

57. .... has been third twice (2 words).

58. Lee asked the .... if he could .... him to the service station.

59. It isn't .... to send a deposit.

60. The policeman had given the boy .... (2 words).

61. Gary Hall had his face .... by a complete stranger.

62. The fireplace wasn't big .... for a man to get down.

63. Mrs. Silva wanted to buy an .... (2 words).

64. .... was discovered in 1789.

65. An Interstate highway will be .... just down the street.

66. A .... gun was used.

67. Condors are .... with extinction.

68. Elvis was .... years old when he died.

69. If he .... older, he'd apply.

70. .... cost two dollars (2 words).

71. The old man said he .... all his life. (3 words).

72. The man in the bar was smoking a ....

73. The police saw the man. He was lying .... a car.

74. She .... to see him in the V.I.P. lounge.

75. The examiner told Marta to .... a picture.

76. There was an .... between the hotel and the beach (2 words).

77. She'd like to have her skirt ....

78. Josh was sitting in a .... (2 words).

79. The Caliph gave Abdul .... to go to Samarra.

80. She went to a new restaurant and said the .... was great.